Arts & Recreational Therapy for Seniors

VOLUME 2

77 ART TEMPLATES TO PRINT

TO USE WITH VOLUME 1 ARTS BOOK

BY

Carol Hill

Coloring Arts

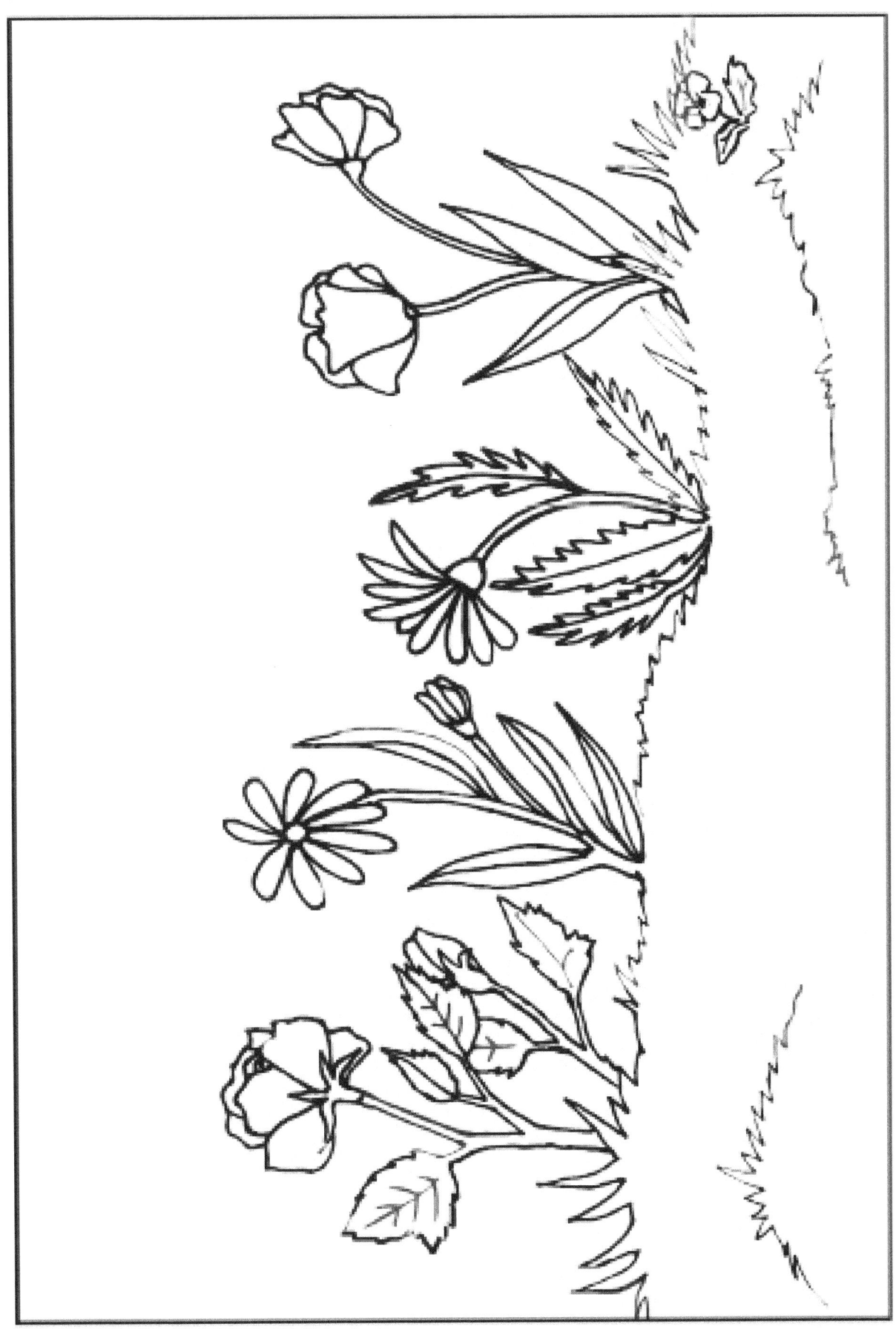

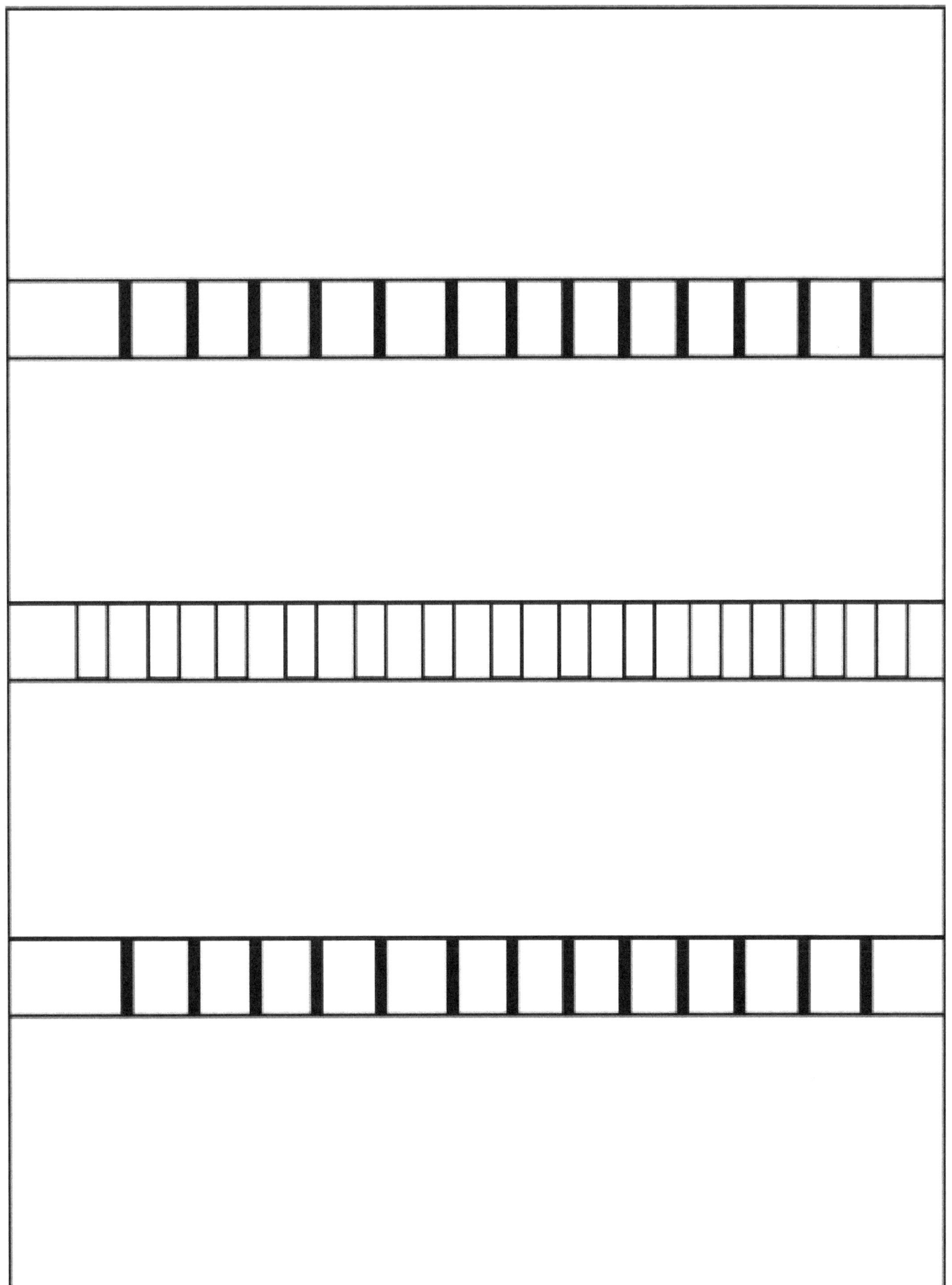

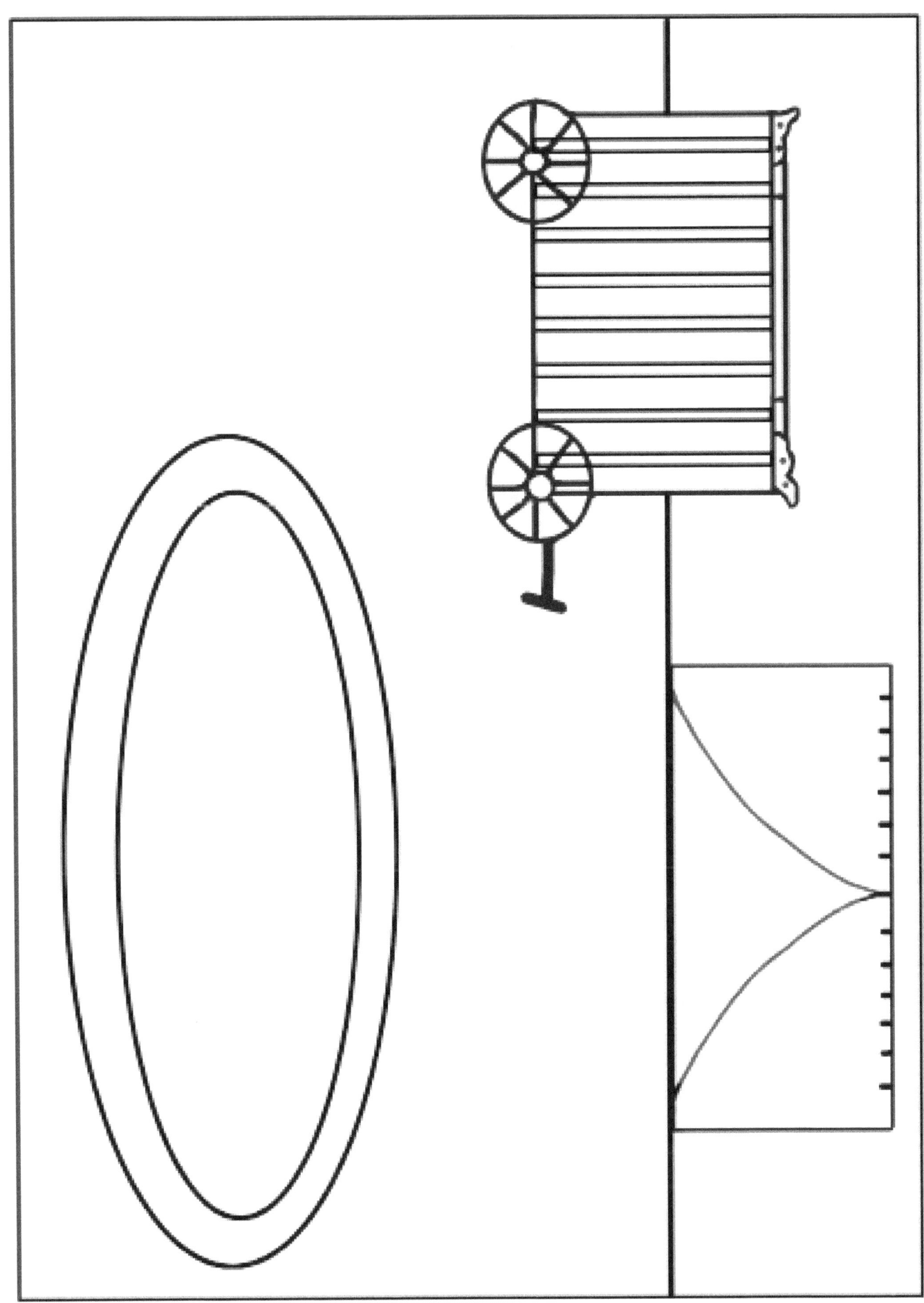

Farm Animals

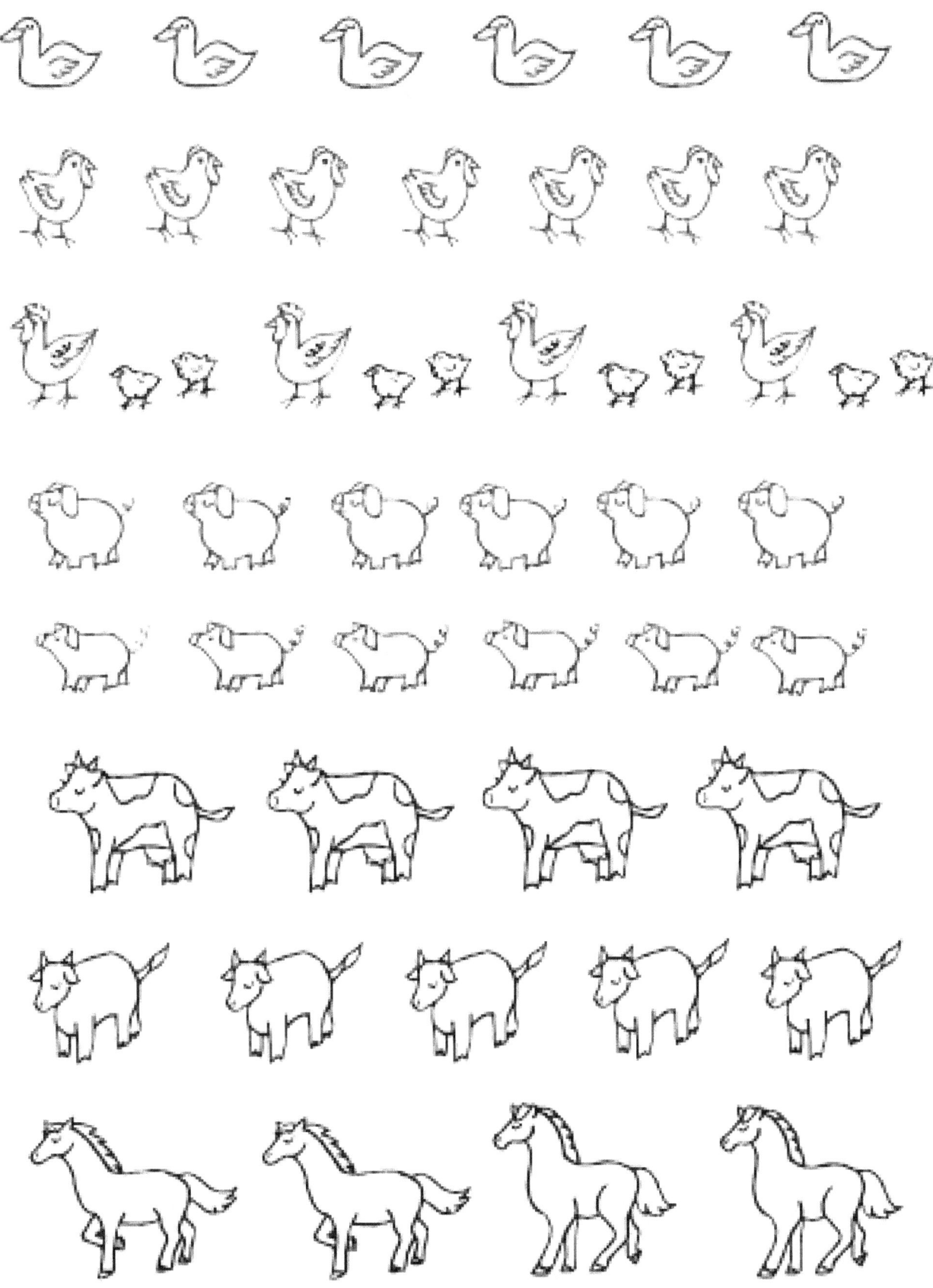

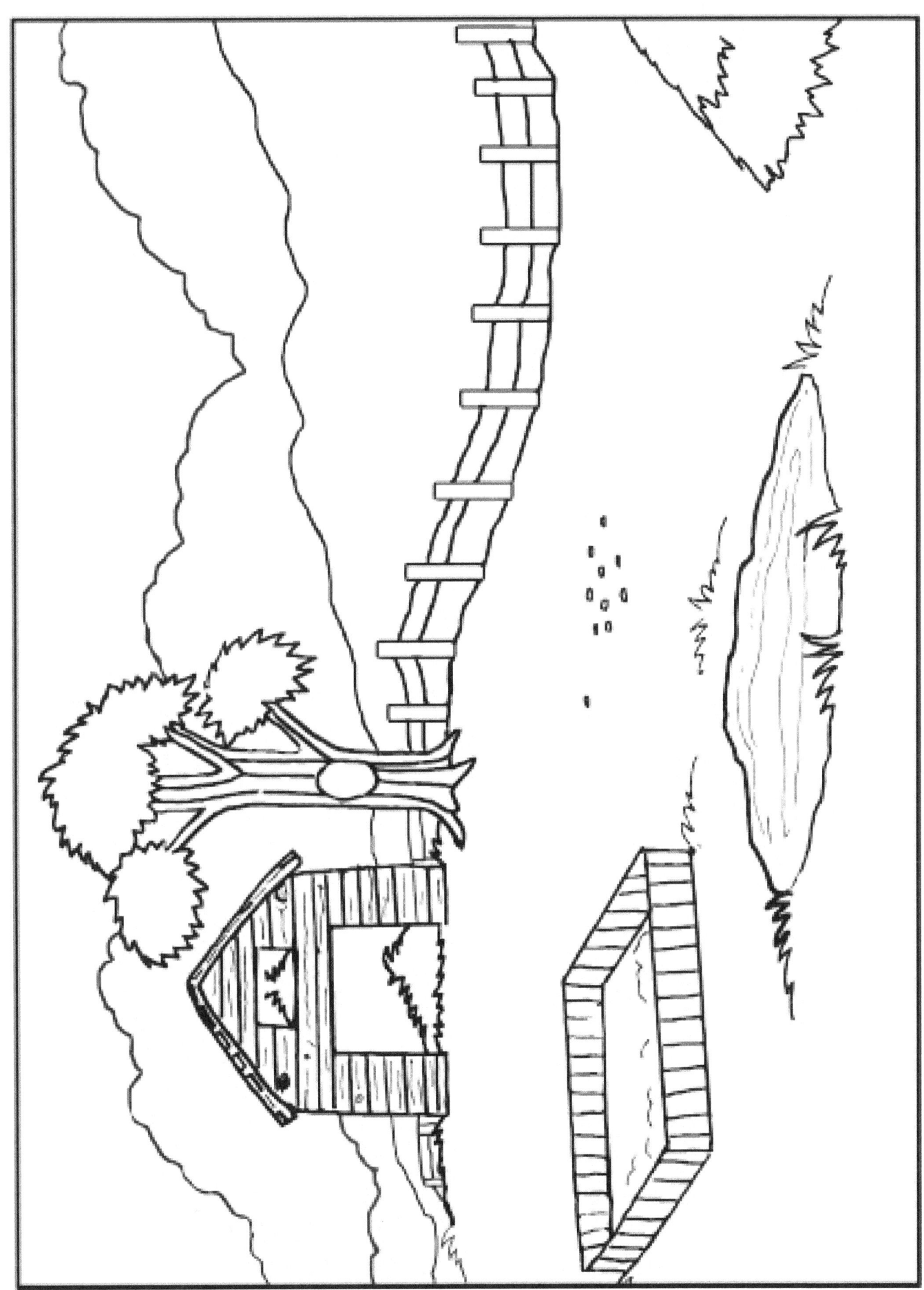

Vegetables

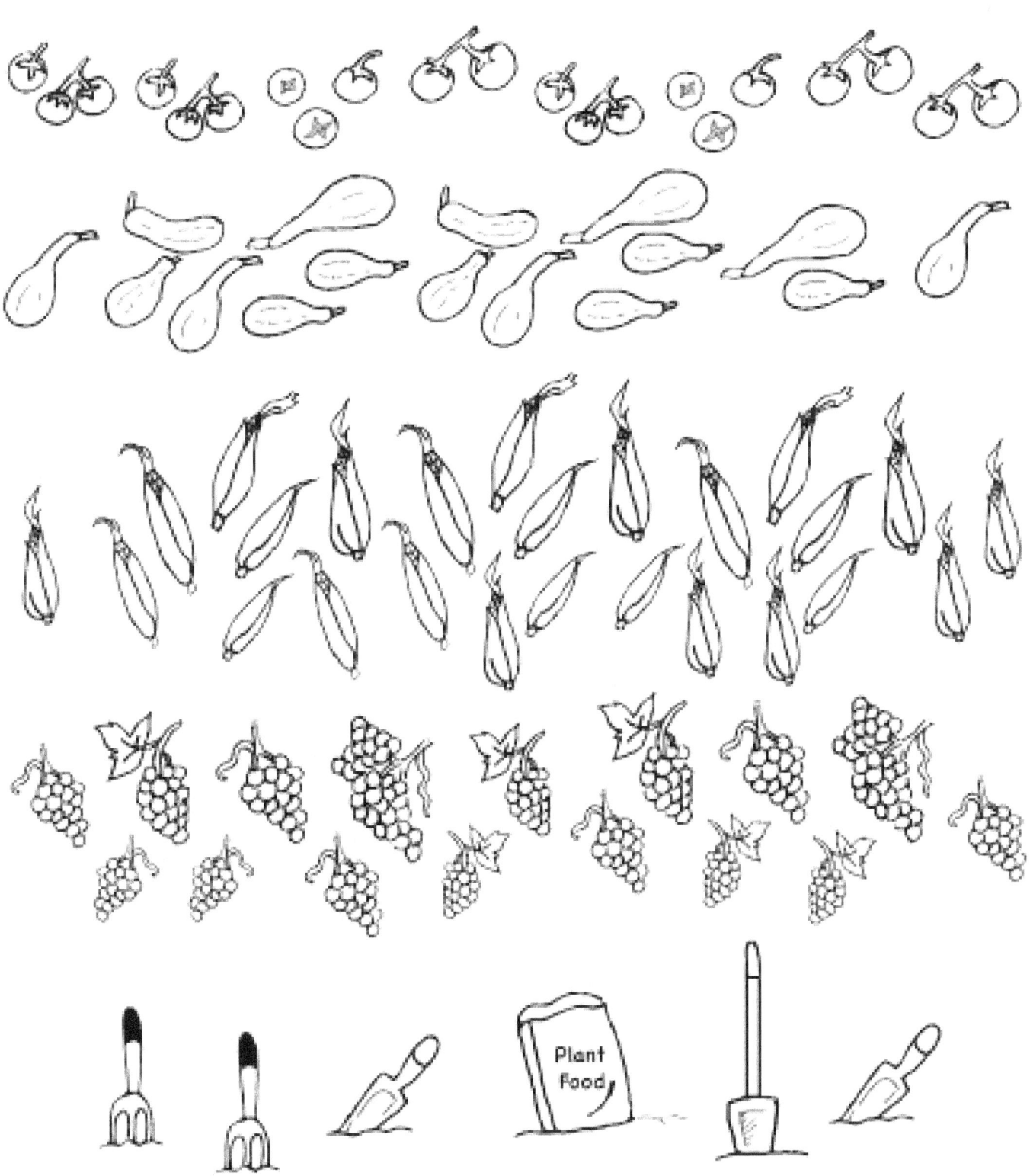

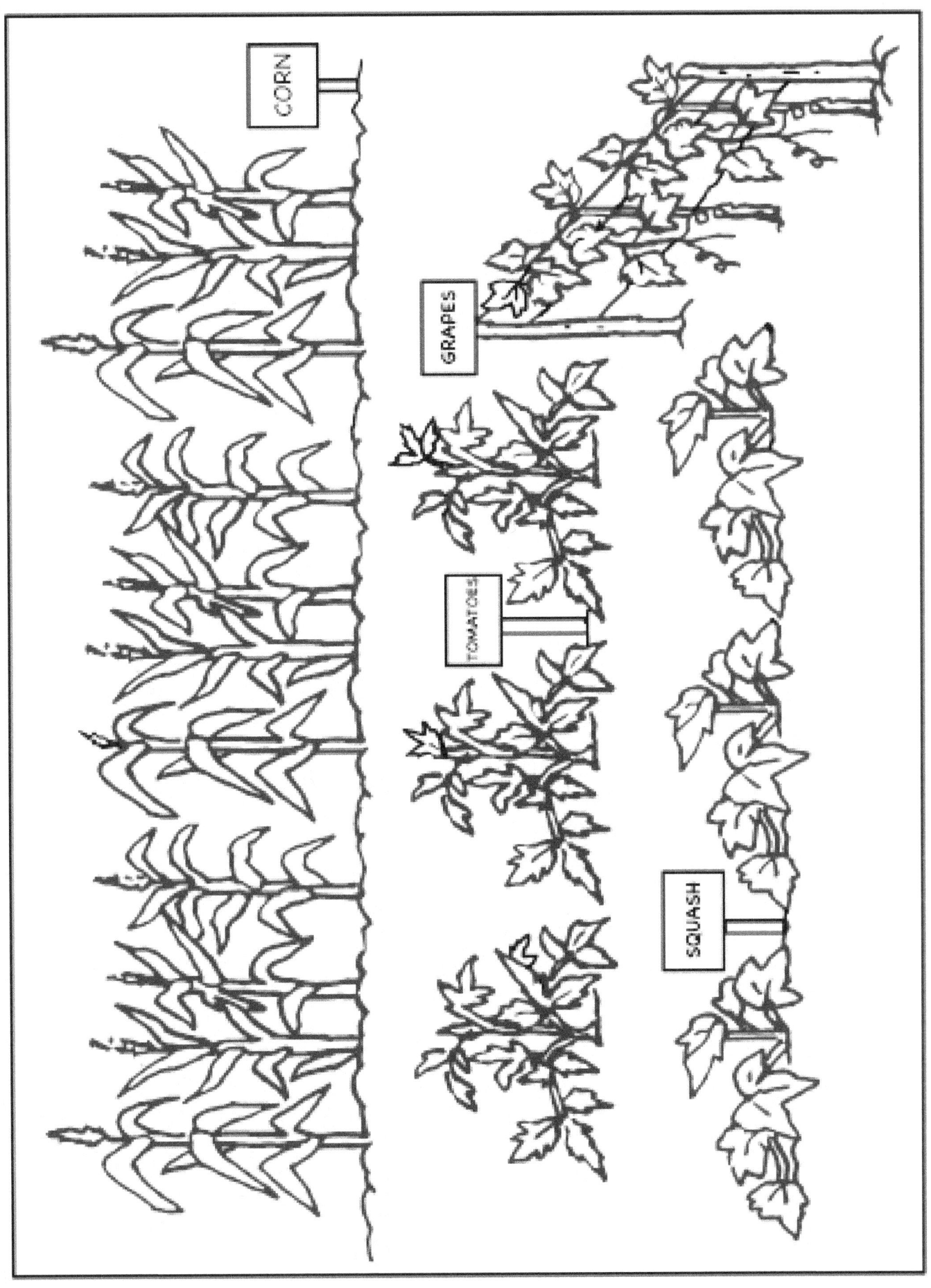

May Flowers

Fish Bowl

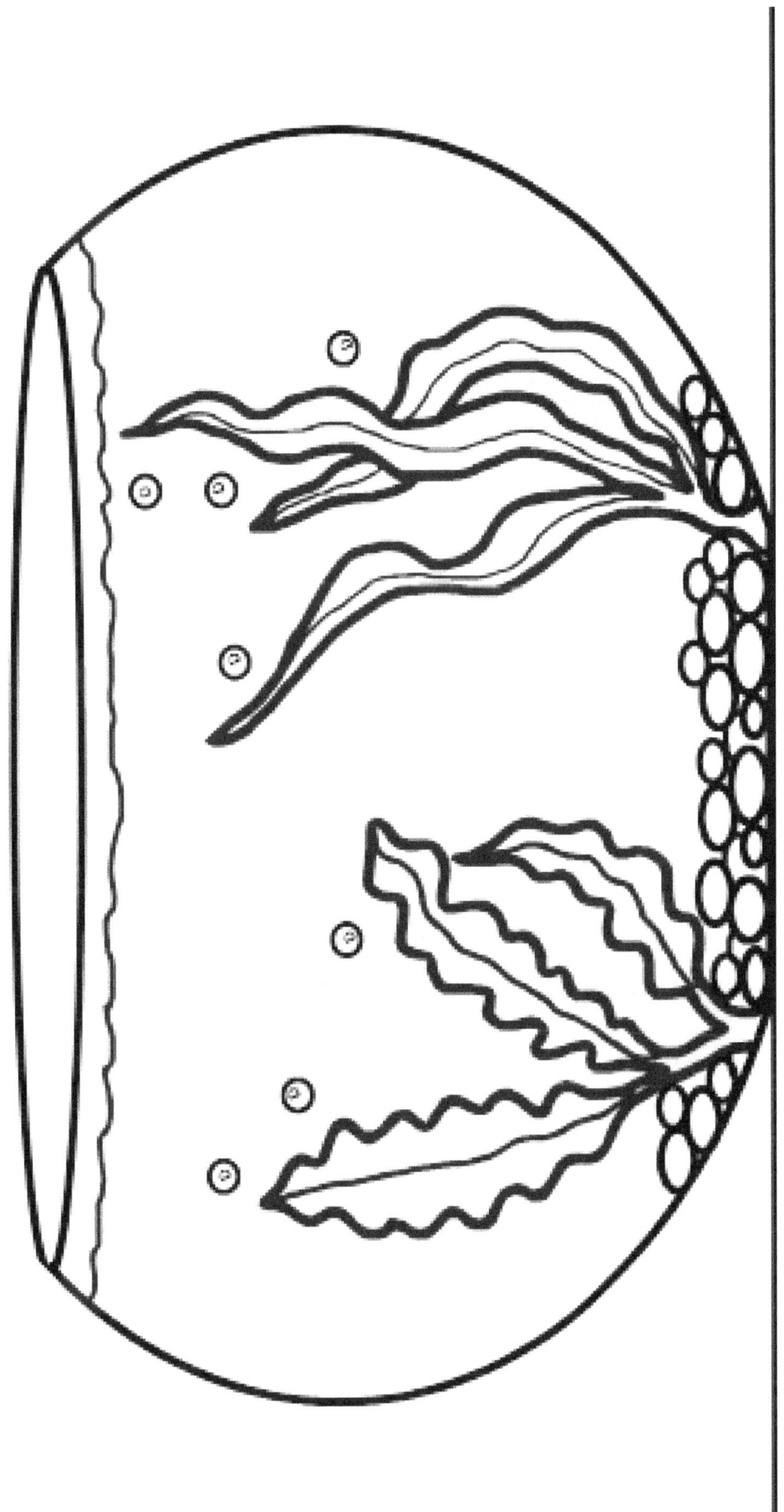

Tropical fish for fish bowl

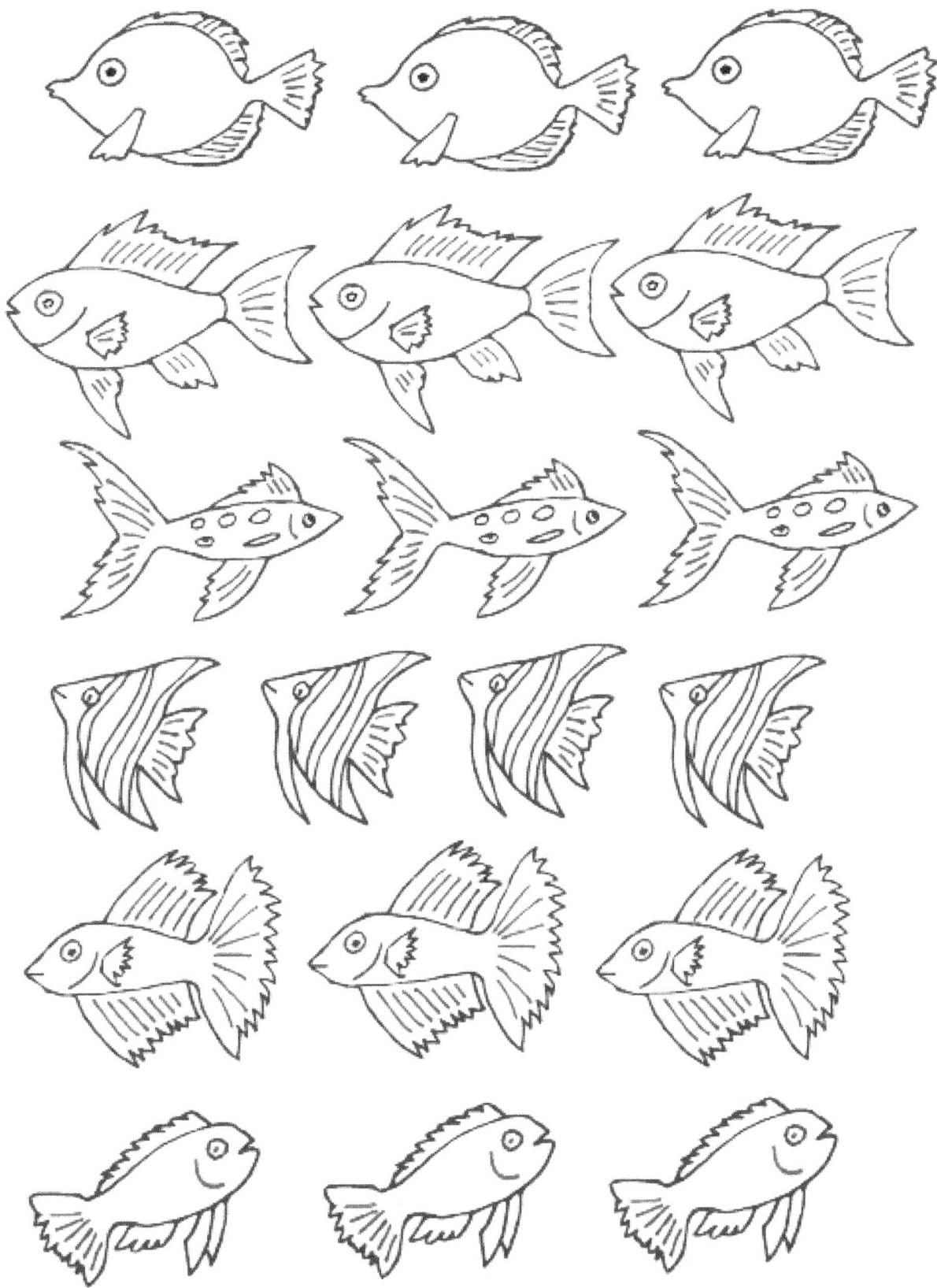

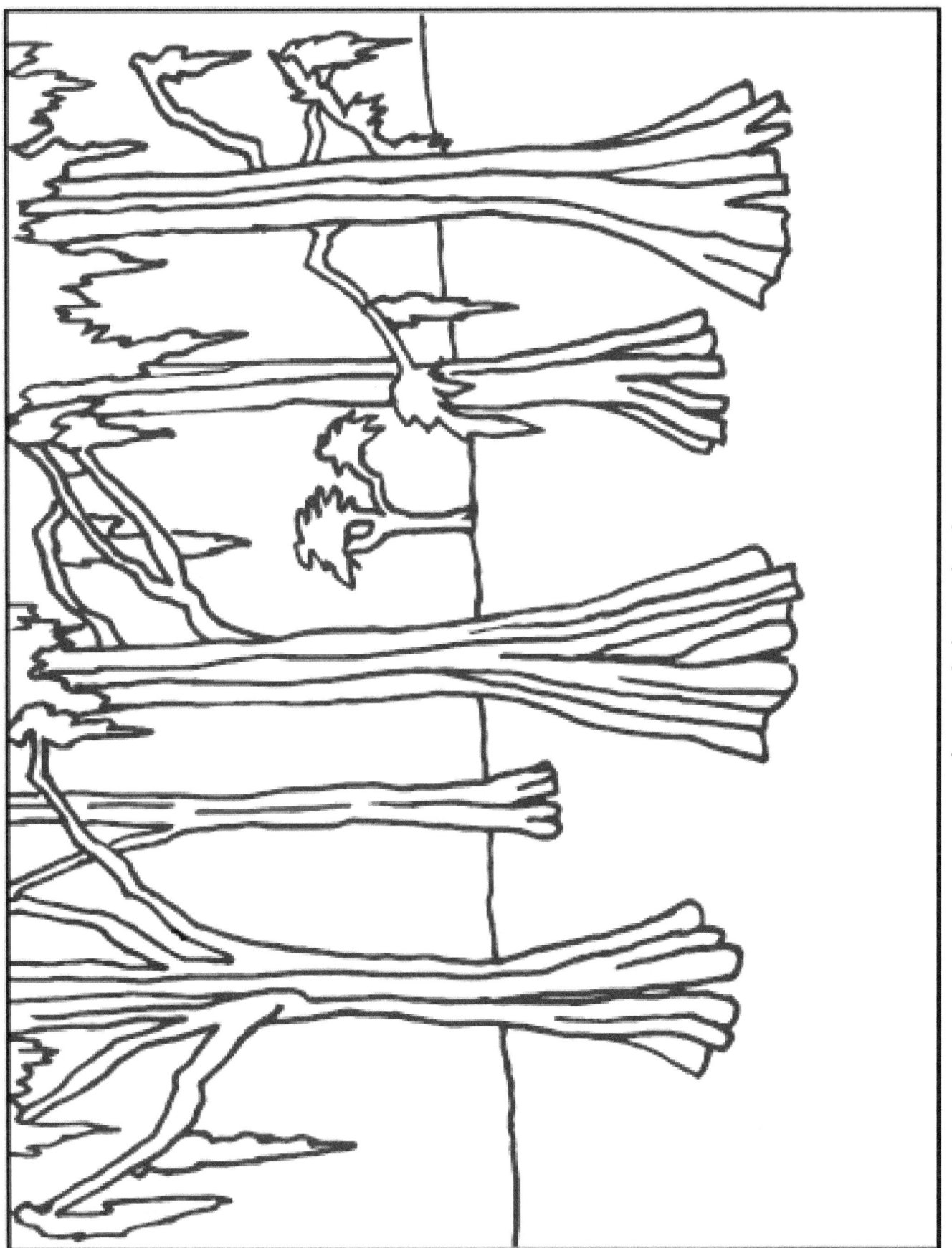

The Everglades in Florida

Flower pattern 2

Fall Tree Pattern

Fall Leaf pattern

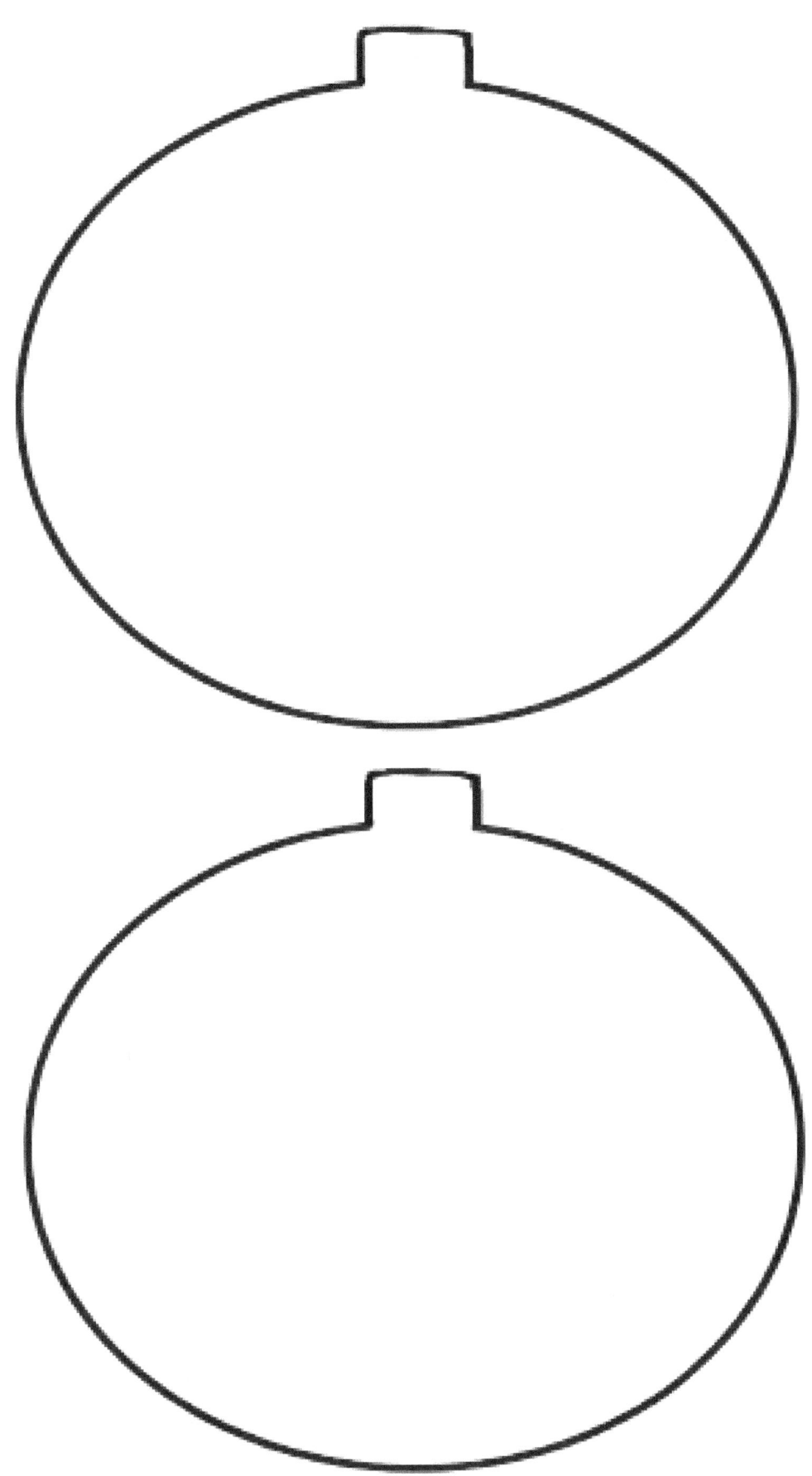

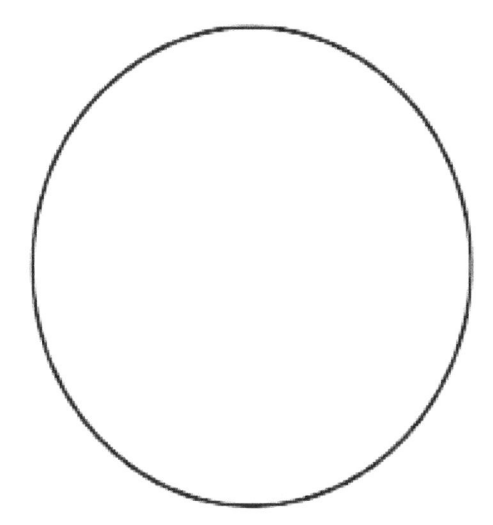

HAPPY HALLOWEEN

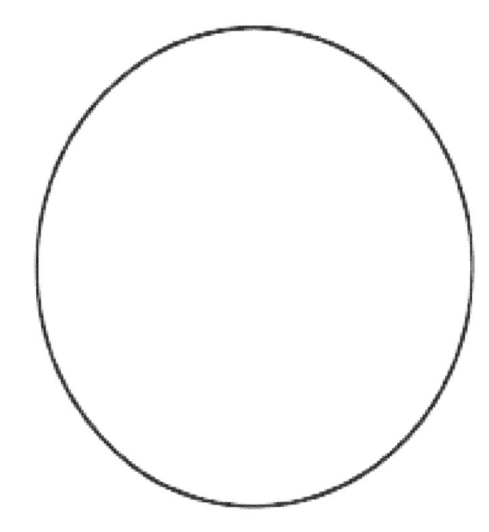

HAPPY HALLOWEEN

HAPPY HALLOWEEN

HAPPY HALLOWEEN

HAPPY HALLOWEEN

HAPPY HALLOWEEN

staple
ribbon here
& tie in back

staple
ribbon here

decorate with sequins, beads or feathers-or glitter

print on heavy, colored paper or construction paper (for printers)

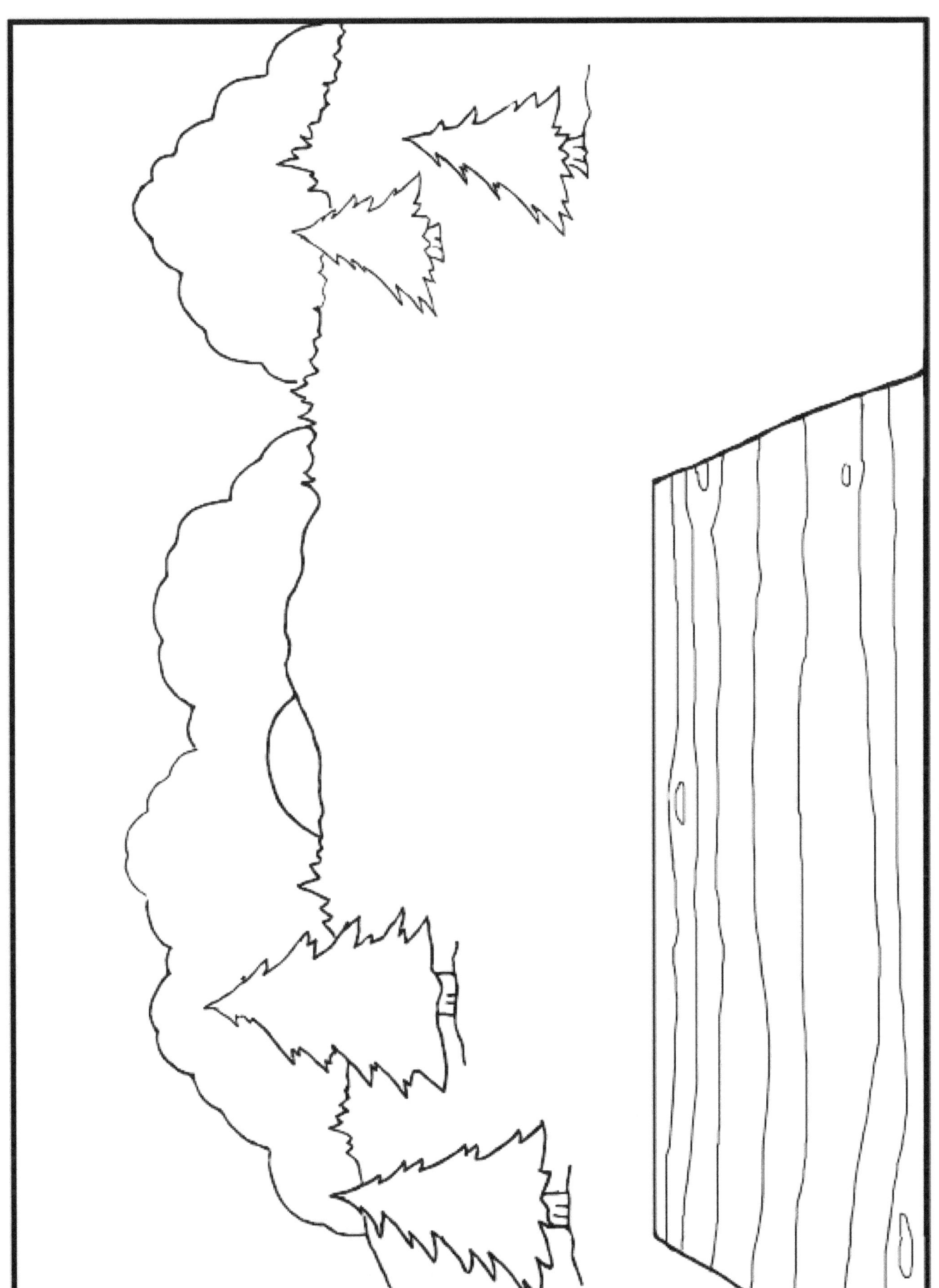

The First Thanksgiving

Turkey Pattern

Happy Thanksgiving

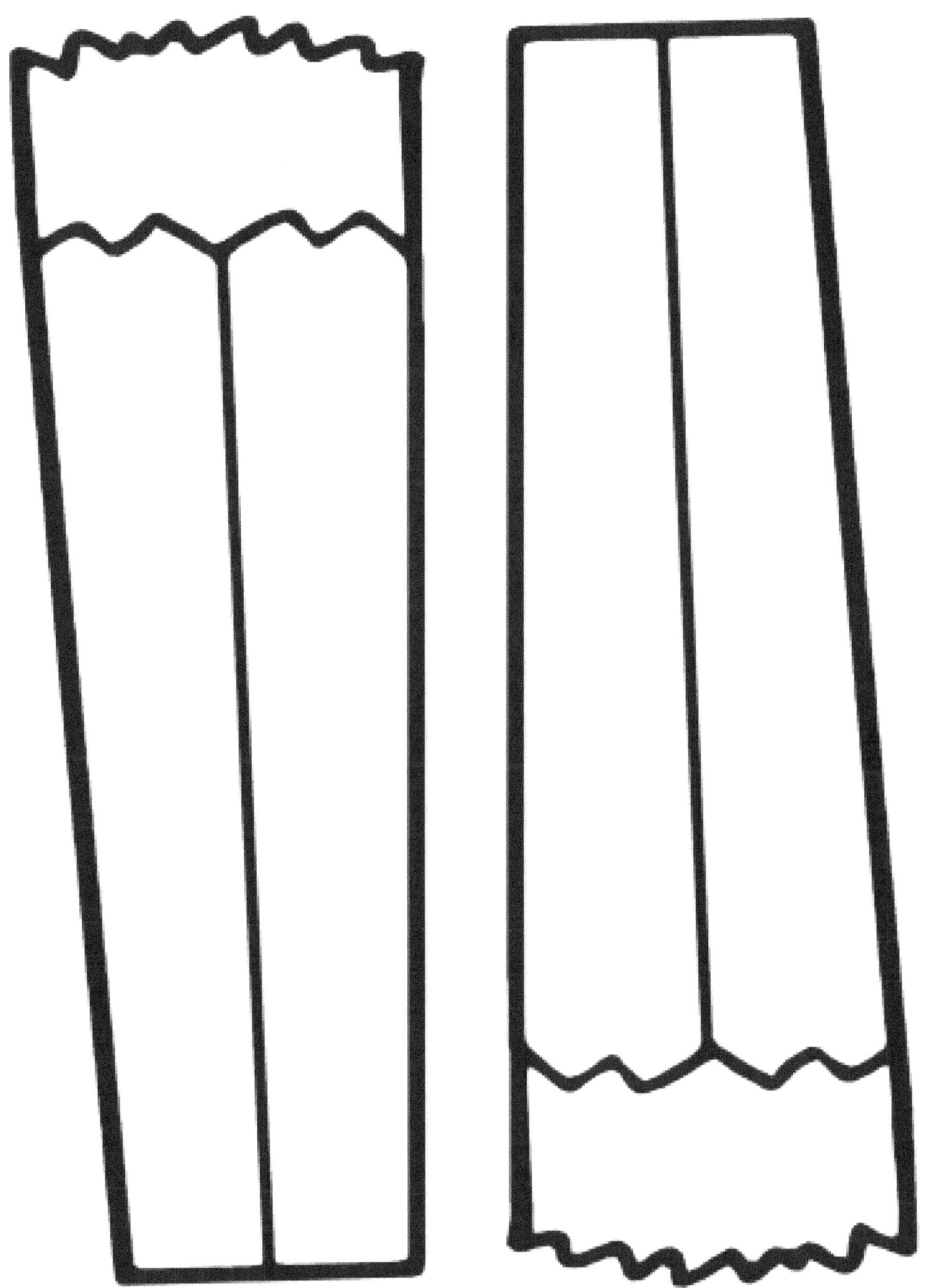

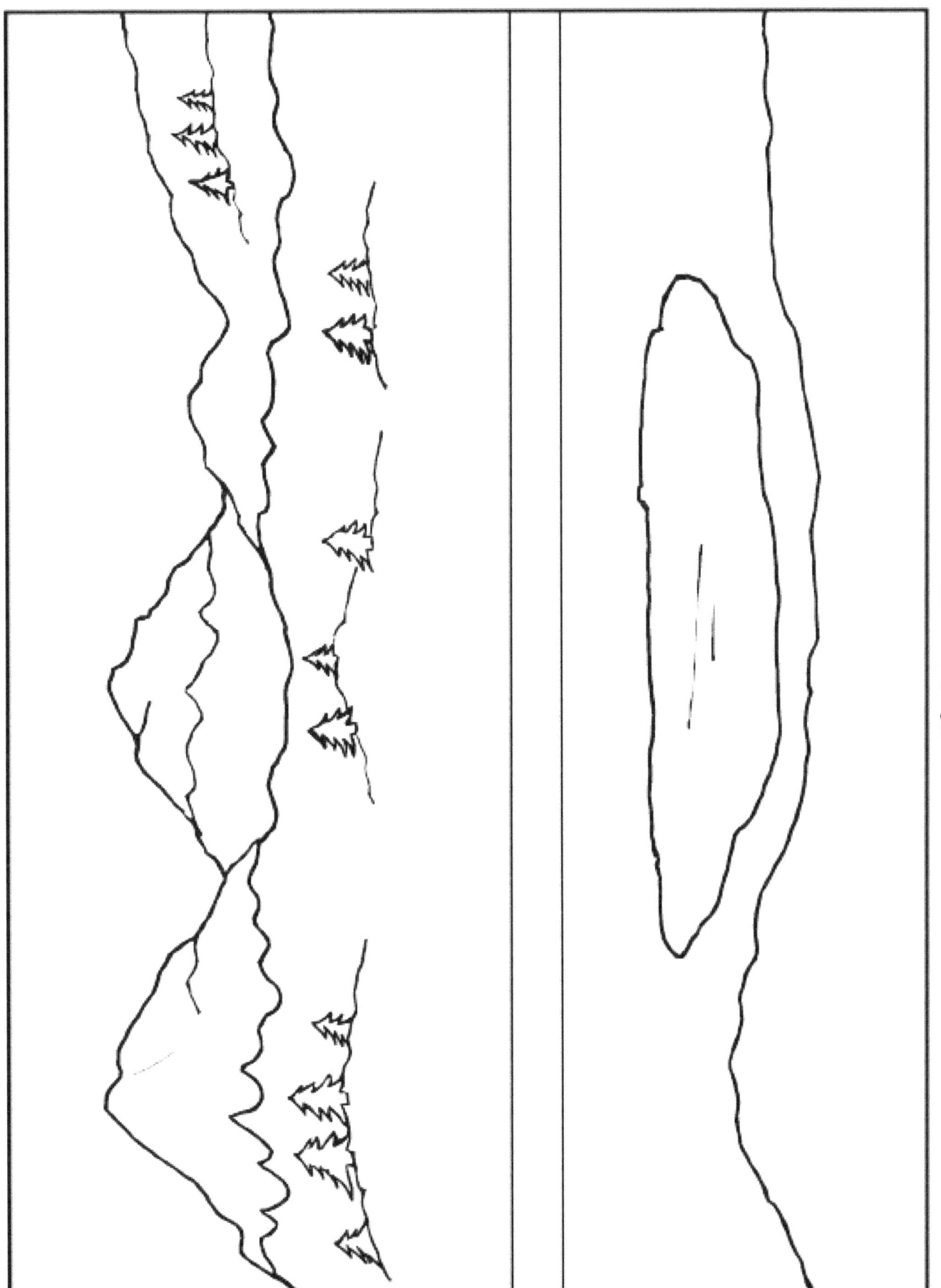

Christmas Towne

Pattern for Gingerbread banner

Frosty The Snowman

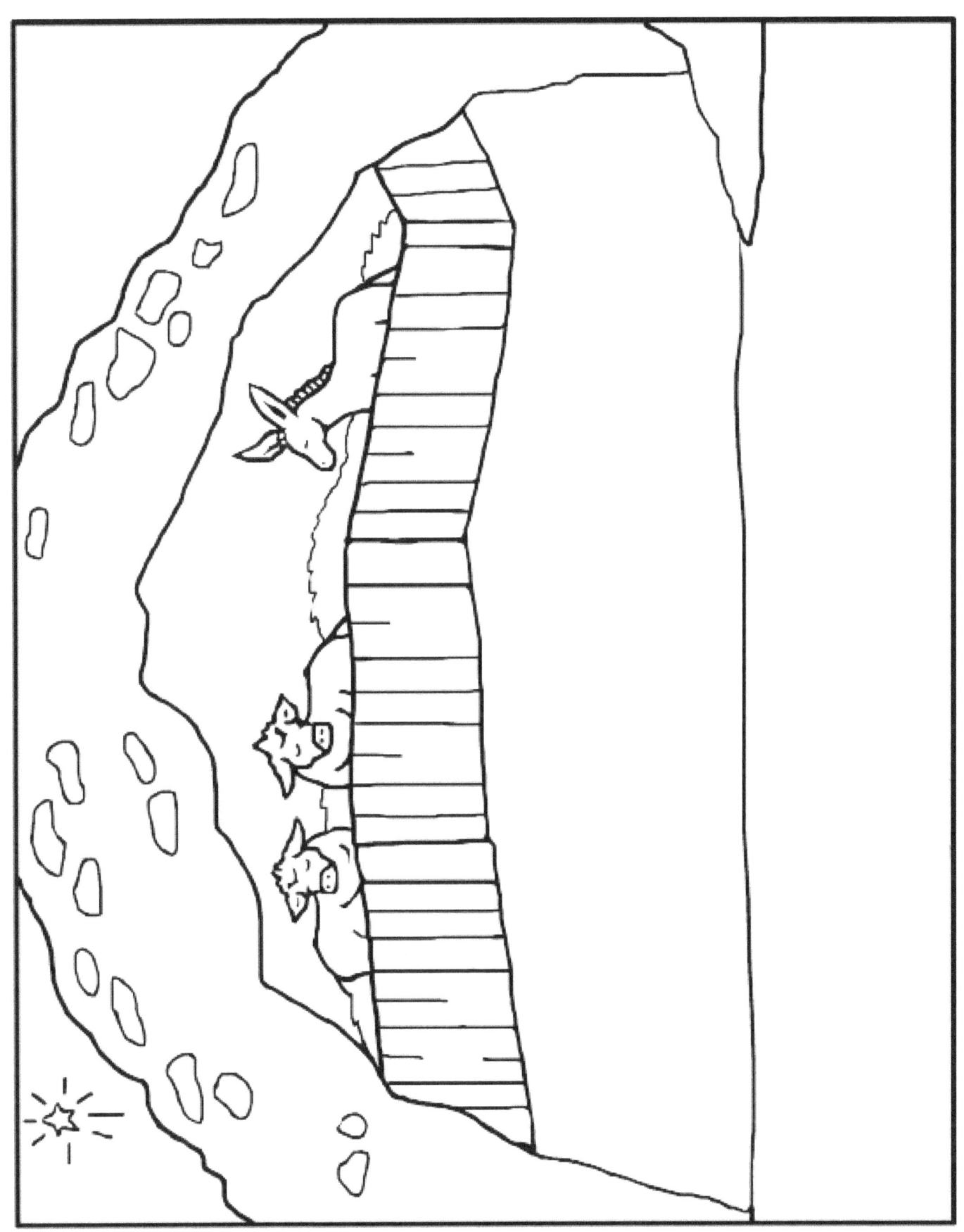

Manger Scene figures

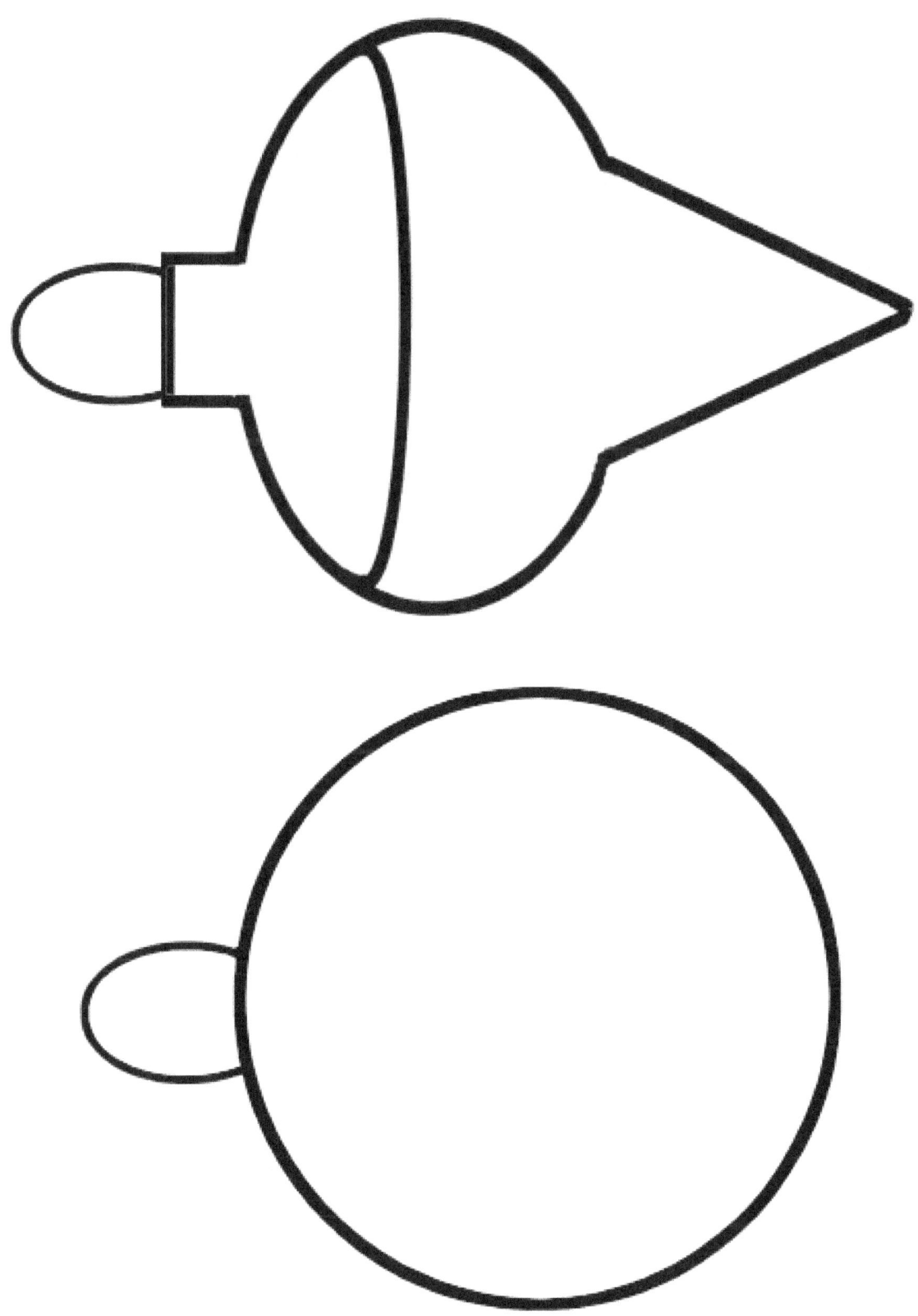

My Family History

By _____

My Family History

Where I was born

About my siblings

About my parents

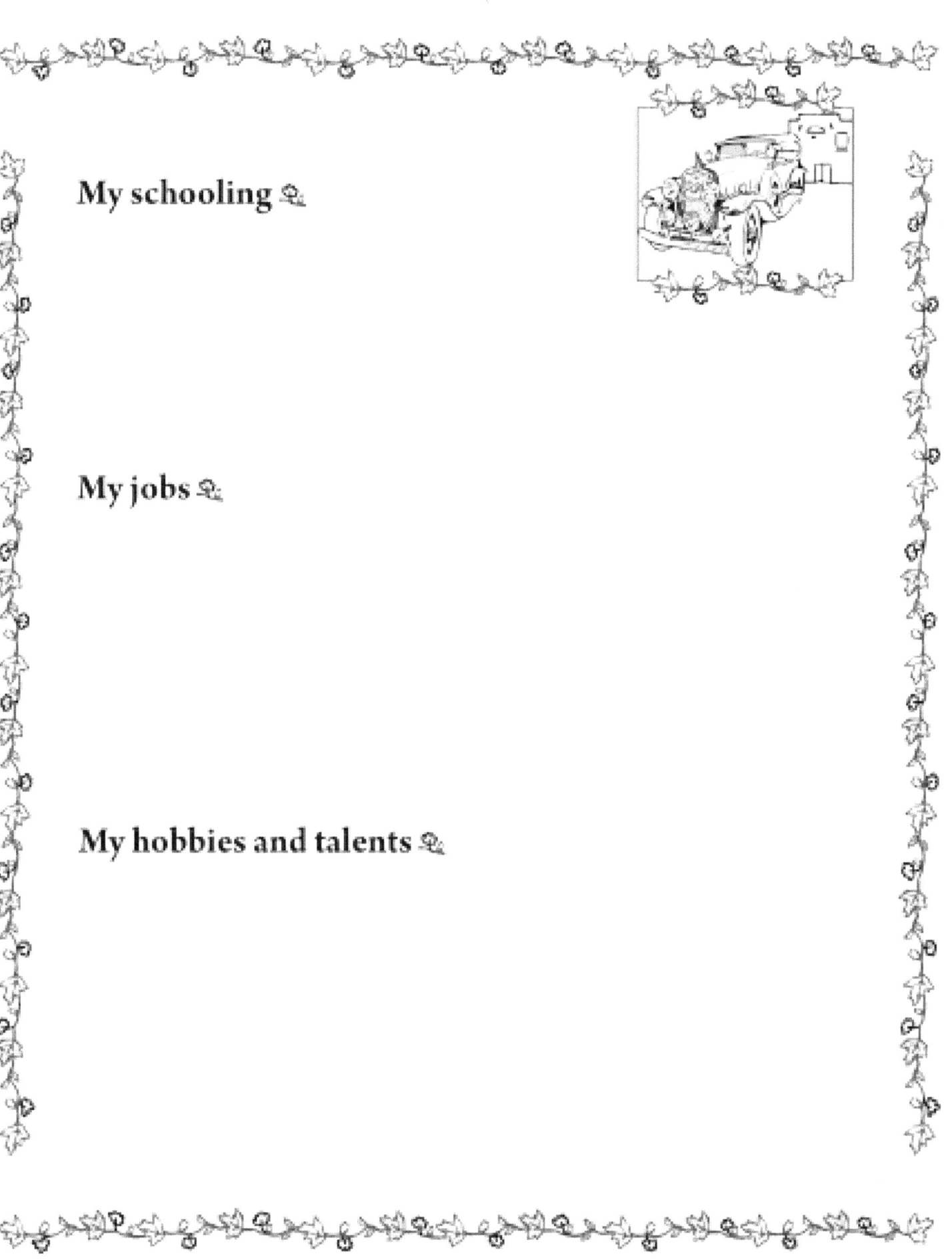

My schooling ❧

My jobs ❧

My hobbies and talents ❧

My marriage ❧

About my husband/wife ❧

About my children ❧

Family fun times

My Family trips

My goals in life

Special things I remember

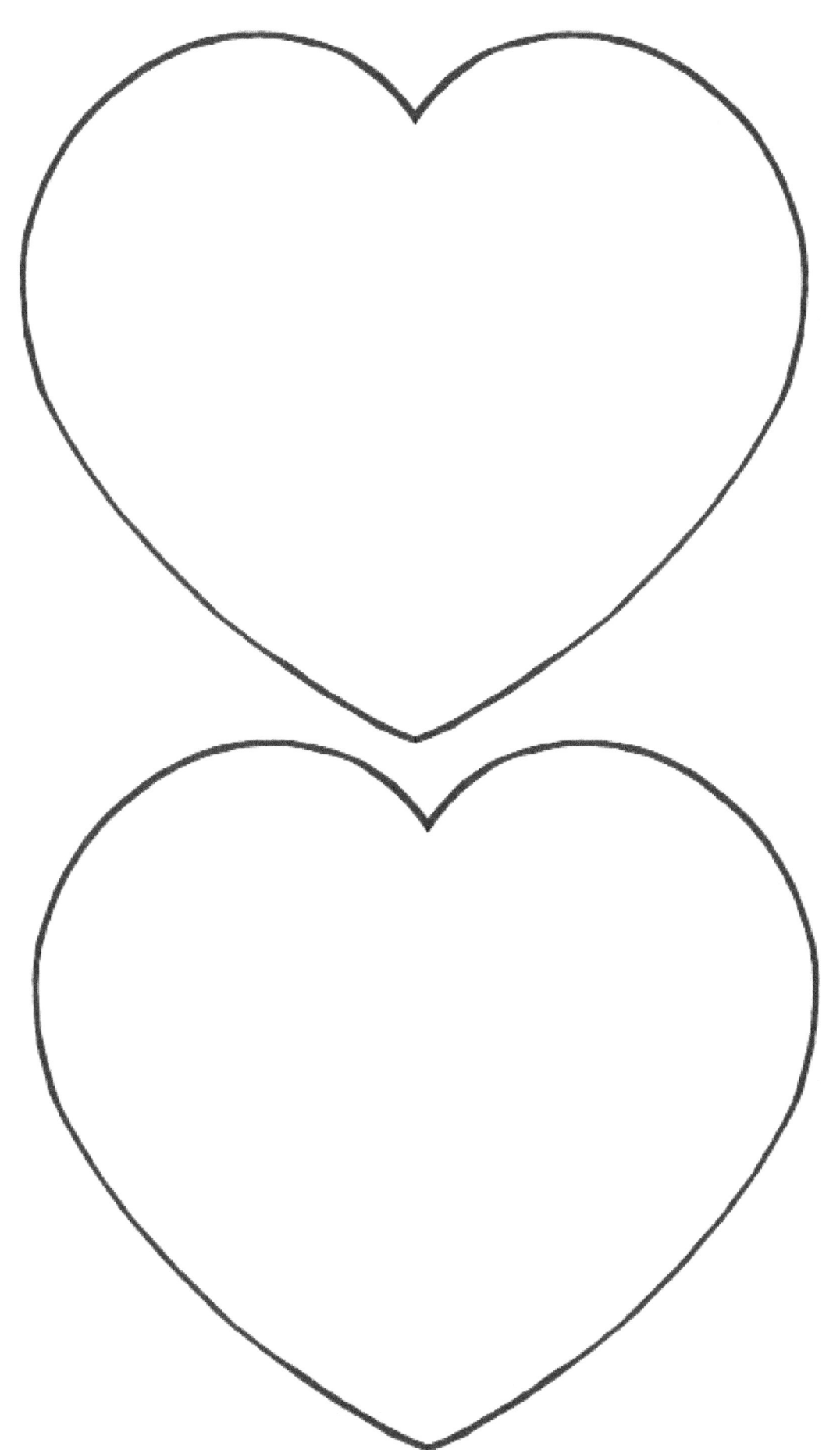

Valentines

Fold colored paper in half and use heart pattern to cut out your hearts-then place lace paper hearts on top and add decorations.

For Valentine Banner -
Cut out large hearts
first in one color and
small hearts in a
different color.
String with twine
and write --I love You
or Be My Valentine, etc.

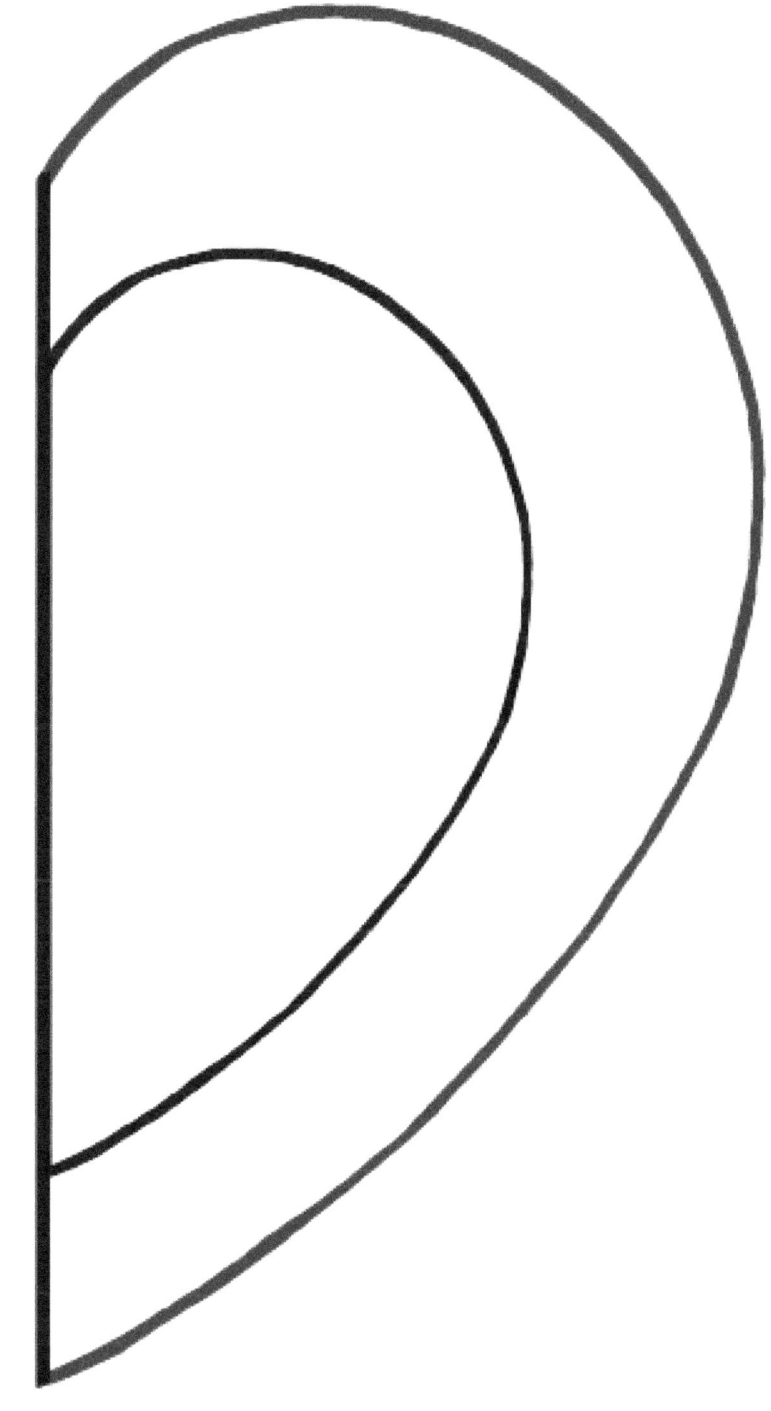

Happy Valentines
Day

Stars for Flag

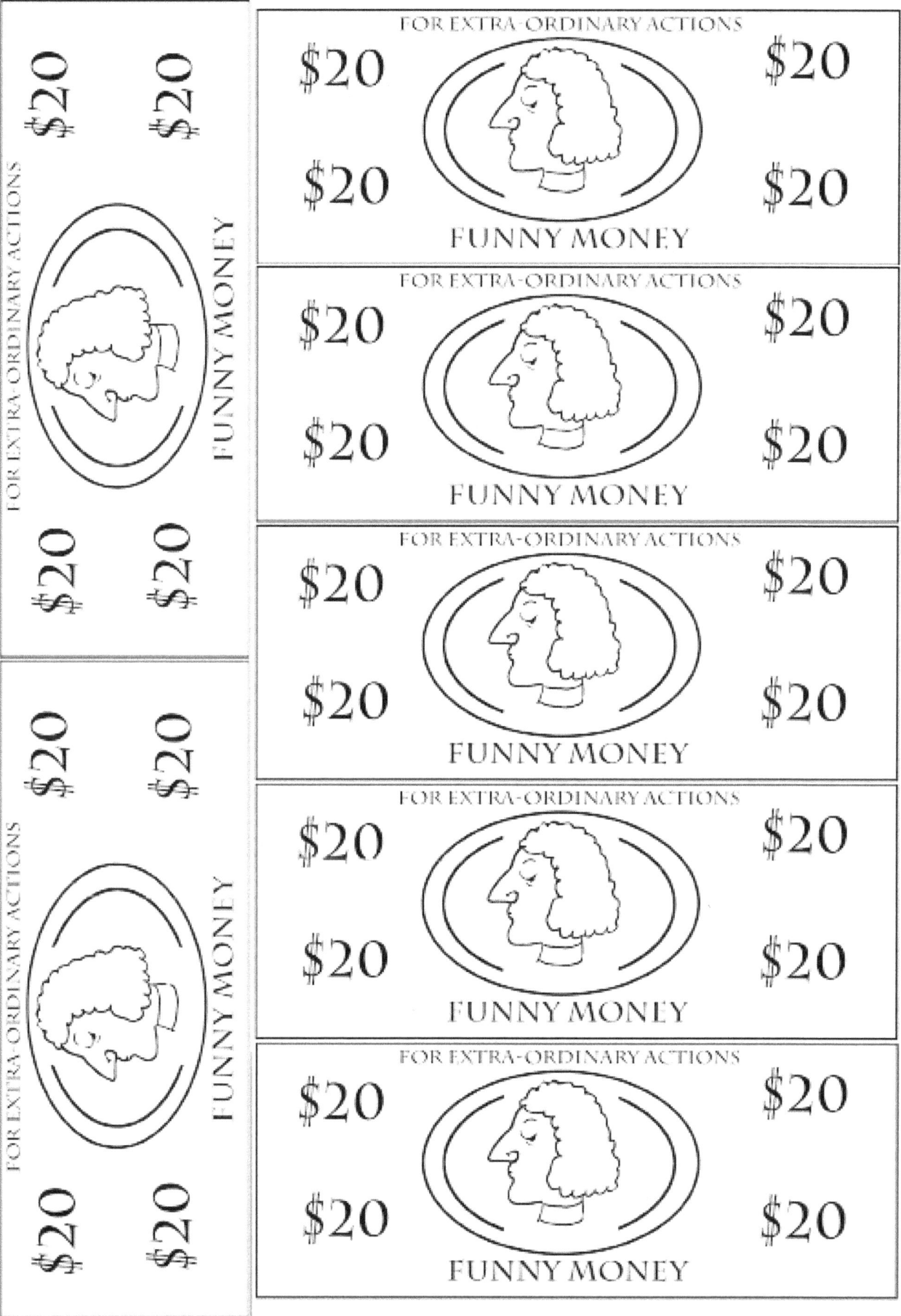

Winter Activity

Presidents Day and Washington's Birthday

1. Have the residents color any of the pictures provided.

2. Talk about our great Presidents. Have the residents tell about their favorite President, and tell why they have chosen him.

4. Have a President's Trivia game--see how many Presidents they can name.

May God Bless Our Great Nation

George Washington

Mount Rushmore

We Honor All Our Great Presidents on This President's Day

CHINESE NEW YEAR

Happy St. Patrick's Day

Wearing of the Green

May The Luck
of The Irish
Be With You

Happy St. Patrick's Day

Pattern for Shamrocks

April Showers Bring May Flowers

Happy Easter

Happy Easter

Happy Easter

Fashion Show - Night 1

Judges Name					Date
Name	Appearance 1 to 10	Personality 1 to 10	Answers 1 to 10	Poise 1 to 10	Comments

Talent Show - Night 2

Name	Personality 1 to 10	Talent 1 to 10	Answers 1 to 10	Comments Things you liked or disliked

Philosophy of Life - Night 3

Name	Personality 1 to 10	Speaking ability 1 to 10	Answers 1 to 10	Comments

Flower Pattern for Spring

Stallions in The Surf

Home On The Range

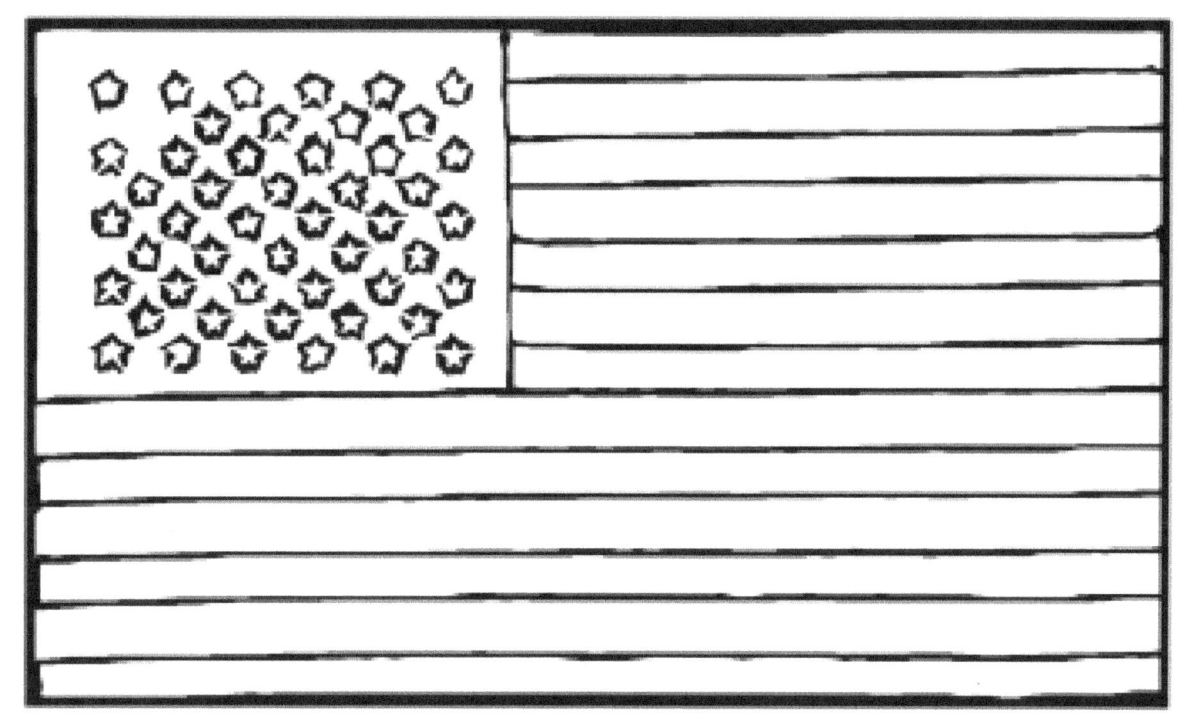

To All The Veterans
That Served Our Country
We
Thank You

patterns to color for veteran's day badges (gold around star and red, white and blue stripes)

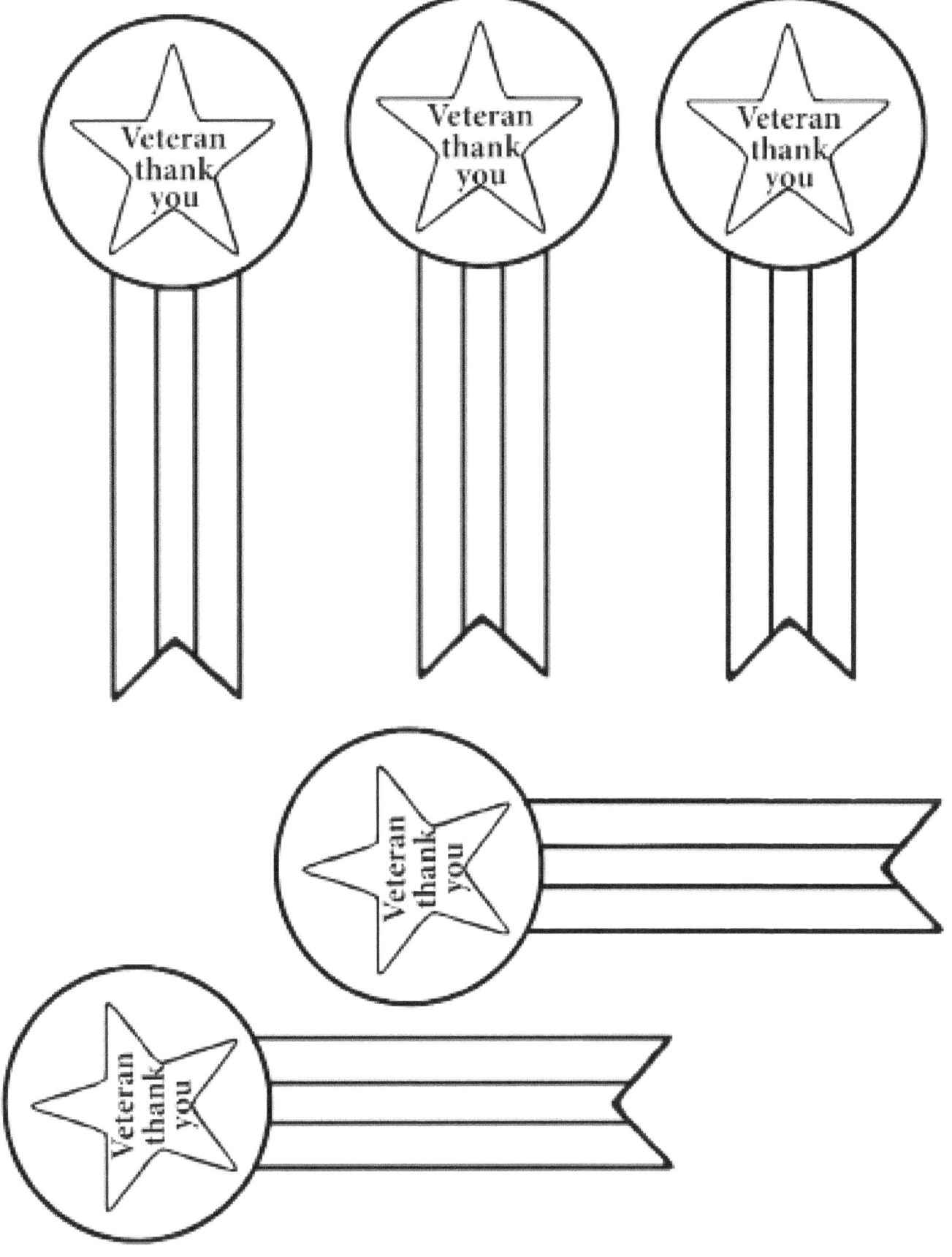

www.ingramcontent.com/pod-product-compliance
Lightning Source LLC
Chambersburg PA
CBHW081214280526
45787CB00006B/2402